HUMANIST MANIFESTOS I AND II

Prometheus Books
923 Kensington Avenue,
Buffalo, New York 14215

Humanist Manifesto I first appeared in *The New Humanist*,
May/June 1933 (Vol. VI, No. 3).
Humanist Manifesto II first appeared in *The Humanist*, Sep-
tember/October 1973 (Vol. XXXIII, No. 5).

ISBN 0-87975-031-6
Printed in the United States of America

Preface

Humanism is a philosophical, religious, and moral point of view as old as human civilization itself. It has its roots in classical China, Greece, and Rome; it is expressed in the Renaissance and the Enlightenment, in the scientific revolution, and in the twentieth century.

Each age seeks to define what its distinctive values are, what it seeks to cherish and enhance. Each age has to contend with alienating and restrictive forces that seek to denigrate the individual, undermine humane values, and suppress social justice.

In the twentieth century, humanist awareness has developed at a rapid pace; yet it has to overcome powerful antihumanist forces that seek to destroy it.

In 1933 a group of thirty-four liberal humanists in the United States defined and enunciated the philosophical and religious principles that seemed to them fundamental. They drafted *Humanist Manifesto I*, which for its time was a radical document. It was concerned with expressing a general religious and philosophical outlook that rejected orthodox and dogmatic positions and provided meaning and direction, unity and purpose to human life. It was committed to reason, science, and democracy.

Humanist Manifesto I, important as it was in its time, has since been superseded by events; though significant, it did not go far enough. It did not and could not address itself to future problems and needs. In recognition of the pressing need for a new, more relevant statement, forty years later *Humanist Manifesto II* was drafted. This more extensive and comprehensive document addresses itself not only to the problems of religion and ethics, but to the pressing issues of civil liberties, equality, democracy, the survival of humankind, world economic growth, population and ecological control, war and peace, and the building of a world community. If the starting point of humanism is the preservation and enhancement of all things human, then what more worthwhile goal than the realization of the human potentiality of each individual and of humanity as a whole? What more

3

pressing need than to recognize in this critical age of modern science and technology that, if no deity will save us, we must save ourselves? It is only by assuming responsibility for the human condition and in marshaling the arts of intelligence that humankind can hope to deal with the emerging problems of the twenty-first century and beyond. If we are to succeed in this venture, must we not abandon the archaic dogmas and ideologies that inhibit creative explorations and solutions?

Humanist Manifesto II was first signed by 114 individuals of prominence and distinction. It has since been endorsed by countless numbers of human beings from all walks of life as a document for our time, committed to both human fulfillment and survival. It is truly worldwide in scope. It seeks to express the longings and aspirations of women as well as men and people of different ethnic and racial origins.

We herein publish both manifestos as working papers, committed to the development of a humanist awareness and an ethical concern. They are presented in a spirit of on-going and cooperative inquiry. They are intended not as new dogmas or credos for an age of confusion, but as the expression of a quest for values and goals that we can work for and that can help us to take new directions. Humanists are committed to building a world that is significant, not only for the individual's quest for meaning, but for the whole of humankind.

Paul Kurtz

4

CONTENTS

Humanist
Manifesto I

The time has come for widespread recognition of the radical changes in religious beliefs throughout the modern world. The time is past for mere revision of traditional attitudes. Science and economic change have disrupted the old beliefs. Religions the world over are under the necessity of coming to terms with new conditions created by a vastly increased knowledge and experience. In every field of human activity, the vital movement is now in the direction of a candid and explicit humanism. In order that religious humanism may be better understood we, the undersigned, desire to make certain affirmations which we believe the facts of our contemporary life demonstrate.

There is great danger of a final, and we believe fatal, identification of the word *religion* with doctrines and methods which have lost their significance and which are powerless to solve the problem of human living in the Twentieth Century. Religions have always been means for realizing the highest values of life. Their end has been accomplished through the interpretation of the total environing situation (theology or world view), the sense of values resulting therefrom (goal or ideal), and the technique (cult) established for realizing the satisfactory life. A change in any of these factors results in alteration of the outward forms of religion. This fact explains the changefulness of religions through the centuries. But through all changes religion itself remains constant in its quest for abiding values, an inseparable feature of human life.

Today man's larger understanding of the universe, his scientific achievements, and his deeper appreciation of brotherhood, have created a situation which requires a new statement of the means and purposes of religion. Such a vital, fearless, and frank religion capable of furnishing adequate social goals and personal satisfactions may appear to many people as a complete break with the past. While this age does owe a vast debt to traditional religions, it is none the less obvious that any religion that can hope to be a synthesizing and dynamic force for today must be shaped for the needs of this age. To establish such a religion is a major necessity of the present. It is a responsibility which rests upon this generation. We therefore affirm the following:

First: Religious humanists regard the universe as self-existing and not created.

Second: Humanism believes that man is a part of nature and that he has emerged as the result of a continuous process.

Third: Holding an organic view of life, humanists find that the traditional dualism of mind and body must be rejected.

Fourth: Humanism recognizes that man's religious culture and civilization, as clearly depicted by anthropology and history, are the product of a gradual development due to his interaction with his natural environment and with his social heritage. The individual born into a particular culture is largely molded to that culture.

Fifth: Humanism asserts that the nature of the universe depicted by modern science makes unacceptable any supernatural or cosmic guarantees of human values. Obviously humanism does not deny the possibility of realities as yet undiscovered, but it does insist that the way to determine the existence and value of any and all realities is by means of intelligent inquiry and by the assessment of their relation to human needs. Religion must formulate its hopes and plans in the light of the scientific spirit and method.

Sixth: We are convinced that the time has passed for theism, deism, modernism, and the several varieties of "new thought."

Seventh: Religion consists of those actions, purposes, and experiences which are humanly significant. Nothing human is alien to the religious. It includes labor, art, science, philosophy, love, friendship, recreation—all that is in its degree expressive of intelligently satisfying human living. The distinction between the sacred and the secular can no longer be maintained.

Eighth: Religious humanism considers the complete realization of human personality to be the end of man's life and seeks its development and fulfillment in the here and now. This is the explanation of the humanist's social passion.

Ninth: In place of the old attitudes involved in worship and prayer the humanist finds his religious emotions expressed in a heightened sense of personal life and in a cooperative effort to promote social well-being.

Tenth: It follows that there will be no uniquely religious emotions and attitudes of the kind hitherto associated with belief in the supernatural.

Eleventh: Man will learn to face the crises of life in terms of his knowledge of their naturalness and probability. Reasonable and manly attitudes will be fostered by education and supported by custom. We assume that humanism will take the path of social and mental hygiene and discourage sentimental and unreal hopes and wishful thinking.

Twelfth: Believing that religion must work increasingly for joy in living, religious humanists aim to foster the creative in man and to encourage achievements that add to the satisfactions of life.

Thirteenth: Religious humanism maintains that all associations and institutions exist for the fulfillment of human life. The intelligent evaluation, transformation, control, and direction of such associations and institutions with a view to the enhancement of human life is the purpose and program of humanism. Certainly religious institutions, their ritualistic forms, ecclesiastical methods, and communal activities must

9

be reconstituted as rapidly as experience allows, in order to function effectively in the modern world.

Fourteenth: The humanists are firmly convinced that existing acquisitive and profit-motivated society has shown itself to be inadequate and that a radical change in methods, controls, and motives must be instituted. A socialized and cooperative economic order must be established to the end that the equitable distribution of the means of life be possible. The goal of humanism is a free and universal society in which people voluntarily and intelligently cooperate for the common good. Humanists demand a shared life in a shared world.

Fifteenth and last: We assert that humanism will: (a) affirm life rather than deny it; (b) seek to elicit the possibilities of life, not flee from it; and (c) endeavor to establish the conditions of a satisfactory life for all, not merely for the few. By this positive *morale* and intention humanism will be guided, and from this perspective and alignment the techniques and efforts of humanism will flow.

So stand the theses of religious humanism. Though we consider the religious forms and ideas of our fathers no longer adequate, the quest for the good life is still the central task for mankind. Man is at last becoming aware that he alone is responsible for the realization of the world of his dreams, that he has within himself the power for its achievement. He must set intelligence and will to the task.

J. A. C. Fagginer Auer
E. Burdette Backus
Harry Elmer Barnes
L. M. Birkhead
Raymond B. Bragg
Edwin Arthur Burtt
Ernest Caldecott
A. J. Carlson

John Dewey
Albert C. Dieffenbach
John H. Dietrich
Bernard Fantus
William Floyd
F. H. Hankins
A. Eustace Haydon
Llewellyn Jones
Robert Morss Lovett
Harold P. Marley
R. Lester Mondale
Charles Francis Potter
John Herman Randall, Jr.
Curtis W. Reese
Oliver L. Reiser
Roy Wood Sellars
Clinton Lee Scott
Maynard Shipley
W. Frank Swift
V. T. Thayer
Eldred C. Vanderlaan
Joseph Walker
Jacob J. Weinstein
Frank S. C. Wicks
David Rhys Williams
Edwin H. Wilson

Humanist Manifesto II

Preface

It is forty years since *Humanist Manifesto I* (1933) appeared. Events since then make that earlier statement seem far too optimistic. Nazism has shown the depths of brutality of which humanity is capable. Other totalitarian regimes have suppressed human rights without ending poverty. Science has sometimes brought evil as well as good. Recent decades have shown that inhuman wars can be made in the name of peace. The beginnings of police states, even in democratic societies, widespread government espionage, and other abuses of power by military, political, and industrial elites, and the continuance of unyielding racism, all present a different and difficult social outlook. In various societies, the demands of women and minority groups for equal rights effectively challenge our generation.

As we approach the twenty-first century, however, an affirmative and hopeful vision is needed. Faith, commensurate with advancing knowledge, is also necessary. In the choice between despair and hope, humanists respond in this *Humanist Manifest II* with a positive declaration for times of uncertainty.

As in 1933, humanists still believe that traditional theism, especially faith in the prayer-hearing God, assumed to love and care for persons, to hear and understand their prayers, and to be able to do something about them, is an unproved and outmoded faith. Salvationism, based on mere affirmation, still appears as harmful, diverting people with false hopes of heaven hereafter. Reasonable minds look to other means for survival.

Those who sign *Humanist Manifesto II* disclaim that they are setting forth a binding credo; their individual views would be stated in widely varying ways. The statement is, however, reaching for vision in a time that needs direction. It is social analysis in an effort at consensus. New statements should be developed to supersede this, but for today it is our conviction that humanism offers an alternative that can serve present-day needs and guide humankind toward the future.

Paul Kurtz   Edwin H. Wilson

The next century can be and should be the humanistic century. Dramatic scientific, technological, and ever-accelerating social and political changes crowd our awareness. We have virtually conquered the planet, explored the moon, overcome the natural limits of travel and communication; we stand at the dawn of a new age, ready to move farther into space and perhaps inhabit other planets. Using technology wisely, we can control our environment, conquer poverty, markedly reduce disease, extend our life-span, significantly modify our behavior, alter the course of human evolution and cultural development, unlock vast new powers, and provide humankind with unparalleled opportunity for achieving an abundant and meaningful life.

The future is, however, filled with dangers. In learning to apply the scientific method to nature and human life, we have opened the door to ecological damage, overpopulation, dehumanizing institutions, totalitarian repression, and nuclear and biochemical disaster. Faced with apocalyptic prophesies and doomsday scenarios, many flee in despair from reason and embrace irrational cults and theologies of withdrawal and retreat.

Traditional moral codes and newer irrational cults both fail to meet the pressing needs of today and tomorrow. False "theologies of hope" and messianic ideologies, substituting new dogmas for old, cannot cope with existing world realities. They separate rather than unite peoples.

Humanity, to survive, requires bold and daring measures. We need to extend the uses of scientific method, not renounce them, to fuse reason with compassion in order to build constructive social and moral values. Confronted by many possible futures, we must decide which to pursue. The ultimate goal should be the fulfillment of the potential for growth in each human personality—not for the favored few, but for all of humankind. Only a shared world and global measures will suffice.

A humanist outlook will tap the creativity of each human being and provide the vision and courage for us to work together. This outlook emphasizes the role human beings can play in their own spheres of action. The decades ahead call for dedicated, clear-minded men and women able to marshal the will, intelligence, and cooperative skills for shaping a desirable future. Humanism can provide the purpose and inspiration that so many seek; it can give personal meaning and significance to human life.

Many kinds of humanism exist in the contemporary world. The varieties and emphases of naturalistic humanism include "scientific," "ethical," "democratic," "religious," and "Marxist" humanism. Free thought, atheism, agnosticism, skepticism, deism, rationalism, ethical culture, and liberal religion all claim to be heir to the humanist tradition. Humanism traces its roots from ancient China, classical Greece and Rome, through the Renaissance and the Enlightenment, to the scientific revolution of the modern world. But views that merely reject theism are not equivalent to humanism. They lack commitment to the positive belief in the possibilities of human progress and to the values central to it Many within religious groups, believing in the future of humanism, now claim humanist credentials. Humanism is an ethical process through which we all can move, above and beyond the divisive particulars, heroic personalities, dogmatic creeds, and ritual customs of past religions or their mere negation.

We affirm a set of common principles that can serve as a basis for united action—positive principles relevant to the present human condition. They are a design for a secular society on a planetary scale.

For these reasons, we submit this new *Humanist Manifesto* for the future of humankind; for us, it is a vision of hope, a direction for satisfying survival.

Religion

First: In the best sense, religion may inspire dedication to the highest ethical ideals. The cultivation of moral devotion and creative imagination is an expression of genuine "spiritual" experience and aspiration.

We believe, however, that traditional dogmatic or authoritarian religions that place revelation, God, ritual, or creed

15

above human needs and experience do a disservice to the human species. Any account of nature should pass the tests of scientific evidence; in our judgment, the dogmas and myths of traditional religions do not do so. Even at this late date in human history, certain elementary facts based upon the critical use of scientific reason have to be restated. We find insufficient evidence for belief in the existence of a supernatural; it is either meaningless or irrelevant to the question of the survival and fulfillment of the human race. As nontheists, we begin with humans not God, nature not deity. Nature may indeed be broader and deeper than we now know; any new discoveries, however, will but enlarge our knowledge of the natural.

Some humanists believe we should reinterpret traditional religions and reinvest them with meanings appropriate to the current situation. Such redefinitions, however, often perpetuate old dependencies and escapisms; they easily become obscurantist, impeding the free use of the intellect. We need, instead, radically new human purposes and goals.

We appreciate the need to preserve the best ethical teachings in the religious traditions of humankind, many of which we share in common. But we reject those features of traditional religious morality that deny humans a full appreciation of their own potentialities and responsibilities. Traditional religions often offer solace to humans, but, as often, they inhibit humans from helping themselves or experiencing their full potentialities. Such institutions, creeds, and rituals often impede the will to serve others. Too often traditional faiths encourage dependence rather than independence, obedience rather than affirmation, fear rather than courage. More recently they have generated concerned social action, with many signs of relevance appearing in the wake of the "God Is Dead" theologies. But we can discover no divine purpose or providence for the human species. While there is much that we do not know, humans are responsible for what we are or will become. No deity will save us; we must save ourselves.

Second: Promises of immortal salvation or fear of eternal damnation are both illusory and harmful. They distract humans from present concerns, from self-actualization, and from rectifying social injustices. Modern science discredits

16

such historic concepts as the "ghost in the machine" and the "separable soul." Rather, science affirms that the human species is an emergence from natural evolutionary forces. As far as we know, the total personality is a function of the biological organism transacting in a social and cultural context. There is no credible evidence that life survives the death of the body. We continue to exist in our progeny and in the way that our lives have influenced others in our culture.

Traditional religions are surely not the only obstacles to human progress. Other ideologies also impede human advance. Some forms of political doctrine, for instance, function religiously, reflecting the worst features of orthodoxy and authoritarianism, especially when they sacrifice individuals on the altar of Utopian promises. Purely economic and political viewpoints, whether capitalist or communist, often function as religious and ideological dogma. Although humans undoubtedly need economic and political goals, they also need creative values by which to live.

Ethics

Third: We affirm that moral values derive their source from human experience. Ethics is *autonomous* and *situational,* needing no theological or ideological sanction. Ethics stems from human need and interest. To deny this distorts the whole basis of life. Human life has meaning because we create and develop our futures. Happiness and the creative realization of human needs and desires, individually and in shared enjoyment, are continuous themes of humanism. We strive for the good life, here and now. The goal is to pursue life's enrichment despite debasing forces of vulgarization, commercialization, bureaucratization, and dehumanization.

Fourth: Reason and intelligence are the most effective instruments that humankind possesses. There is no substitute: neither faith nor passion suffices in itself. The controlled use of scientific methods, which have transformed the natural and social sciences since the Renaissance, must be extended further in the solution of human problems. But reason must be tempered by humility, since no group has a monopoly of wisdom or virtue. Nor is there any guarantee that all problems can be solved or all questions answered. Yet critical intelligence, infused by a sense of human caring, is the best method that humanity has for resolving problems. Reason should be balanced with compassion and empathy and the whole person fulfilled. Thus, we are not advocating the use of scientific intelligence independent of or in opposition to emotion, for we believe in the cultivation of feeling and love. As science pushes back the boundary of the known, one's sense of wonder is continually renewed, and art, poetry, and music find their places, along with religion and ethics.

The Individual

Fifth: The preciousness and dignity of the individual person is a central humanist value. Individuals should be encouraged to realize their own creative talents and desires. We reject all religious, ideological, or moral codes that denigrate the individual, suppress freedom, dull intellect, dehumanize personality. We believe in maximum individual autonomy consonant with social responsibility. Although science can account for the causes of behavior, the possibilities of individual *freedom of choice* exist in human life and should be increased.

Sixth: In the area of sexuality, we believe that intolerant attitudes, often cultivated by orthodox religions and puritanical cultures, unduly repress sexual conduct. The right to birth control, abortion, and divorce should be recognized. While we do not approve of exploitive, denigrating forms of sexual expression, neither do we wish to prohibit, by law or social sanction, sexual behavior between consenting adults. The many varieties of sexual exploration should not in themselves be considered "evil." Without countenancing mindless permissiveness or unbridled promiscuity, a civilized society should be a *tolerant* one. Short of harming others or compelling them to do likewise, individuals should be permitted to express their sexual proclivities and pursue their life-styles as they desire. We wish to cultivate the development of a responsible attitude toward sexuality, in which humans are not exploited as sexual objects, and in which intimacy, sensitivity,

18

respect, and honesty in interpersonal relations are encouraged. Moral education for children and adults is an important way of developing awareness and sexual maturity.

Democratic Society

Seventh: To enhance freedom and dignity the individual must experience a full range of *civil liberties* in all societies. This includes freedom of speech and the press, political democracy, the legal right of opposition to governmental policies, fair judicial process, religious liberty, freedom of association, and artistic, scientific, and cultural freedom. It also includes a recognition of an individual's right to die with dignity, euthanasia, and the right to suicide. We oppose the increasing invasion of privacy, by whatever means, in both totalitarian and democratic societies. We would safeguard, extend, and implement the principles of human freedom evolved from the *Magna Carta* to the *Bill of Rights,* the *Rights of Man,* and the *Universal Declaration of Human Rights.*

Eighth: We are committed to an open and democratic society. We must extend *participatory democracy* in its true sense to the economy, the school, the family, the workplace, and voluntary associations. Decision-making must be decentralized to include widespread involvement of people at all levels—social, political, and economic. All persons should have a voice in developing the values and goals that determine their lives. Institutions should be responsive to expressed desires and needs. The conditions of work, education, devotion, and play should be humanized. Alienating forces should be modified or eradicated and bureaucratic structures should be held to a minimum. People are more important than decalogues, rules, proscriptions, or regulations.

Ninth: The separation of church and state and the separation of ideology and state are imperatives. The state should encourage maximum freedom for different moral, political, religious, and social values in society. It should not favor any particular religious bodies through the use of public

19

monies, nor espouse a single ideology and function thereby as an instrument of propaganda or oppression, particularly against dissenters.

Tenth: Humane societies should evaluate economic systems not by rhetoric or ideology, but by whether or not they *increase economic well-being* for all individuals and groups, minimize poverty and hardship, increase the sum of human satisfaction, and enhance the quality of life. Hence the door is open to alternative economic systems. We need to democratize the economy and judge it by its responsiveness to human needs, testing results in terms of the common good.

Eleventh: The principle of moral equality must be furthered through elimination of all discrimination based upon race, religion, sex, age, or national origin. This means equality of opportunity and recognition of talent and merit. Individuals should be encouraged to contribute to their own betterment. If unable, then society should provide means to satisfy their basic economic, health, and cultural needs, including, wherever resources make possible, a minimum guaranteed annual income. We are concerned for the welfare of the aged, the infirm, the disadvantaged, and also for the outcasts—the mentally retarded, abandoned or abused children, the handicapped, prisoners, and addicts—for *all* who are neglected or ignored by society. Practicing humanists should make it their vocation to humanize personal relations.

We believe in the *right to universal education.* Everyone has a right to the cultural opportunity to fulfill his or her unique capacities and talents. The schools should foster satisfying and productive living. They should be open at all levels to any and all; the achievement of excellence should be encouraged. Innovative and experimental forms of education are to be welcomed. The energy and idealism of the young deserve to be appreciated and channeled to constructive purposes.

We deplore racial, religious, ethnic, or class antagonisms. Although we believe in cultural diversity and encourage racial and ethnic pride, we reject separations which promote alienation and set people and groups against each other; we envision an *integrated* community where people have a maximum opportunity for free and voluntary association.

20

We are *critical of sexism or sexual chauvinism*—male or female. We believe in equal rights for both women and men to fulfill their unique careers and potentialities as they see fit, free of invidious discrimination.

World Community

Twelfth: We deplore the division of humankind on nationalistic grounds. We have reached a turning point in human history where the best option is to *transcend the limits of national sovereignty* and to move toward the building of a world community in which all sectors of the human family can participate. Thus we look to the development of a system of world law and a world order based upon transnational federal government. This would appreciate cultural pluralism and diversity. It would not exclude pride in national origins and accomplishments nor the handling of regional problems on a regional basis. Human progress, however, can no longer be achieved by focusing on one section of the world, Western or Eastern, developed or underdeveloped. For the first time in human history, no part of humankind can be isolated from any other. Each person's future is in some way linked to all. We thus reaffirm a commitment to the building of world community, at the same time recognizing that this commits us to some hard choices.

Thirteenth: This world community must *renounce the resort to violence and force* as a method of solving international disputes. We believe in the peaceful adjudication of differences by international courts and by the development of the arts of negotiation and compromise. War is obsolete. So is the use of nuclear, biological, and chemical weapons. It is a planetary imperative to reduce the level of military expenditures and turn these savings to peaceful and people-oriented uses.

Fourteenth: The world community must engage in *cooperative planning* concerning the use of rapidly depleting resources. The planet earth must be considered a single *ecosystem.* Ecological damage, resource depletion, and excessive population growth must be checked by international concord. The cultivation and conservation of nature is a moral value; we should perceive ourselves as integral to the sources of our being in nature. We must free our world from needless pollution and waste, responsibly guarding and creating wealth, both natural and human. Exploitation of natural resources, uncurbed by social conscience, must end.

Fifteenth: The problems of *economic growth and development* can no longer be resolved by one nation alone; they are worldwide in scope. It is the moral obligation of the developed nations to provide—through an international authority that safeguards human rights—massive technical, agricultural, medical, and economic assistance, including birth control techniques, to the developing portions of the globe. World poverty must cease. Hence extreme disproportions in wealth, income, and economic growth should be reduced on a worldwide basis.

Sixteenth: Technology is a vital key to human progress and development. We deplore any neo-romantic efforts to condemn indiscriminately all technology and science or to counsel retreat from its further extension and use for the good of humankind. We would resist any moves to censor basic scientific research on moral, political, or social grounds. Technology must, however, be carefully judged by the consequences of its use; harmful and destructive changes should be avoided. We are particularly disturbed when technology and bureaucracy control, manipulate, or modify human beings without their consent. Technological feasibility does not imply social or cultural desirability.

Seventeenth: We must expand communication and transportation across frontiers. Travel restrictions must cease. The world must be open to diverse political, ideological, and moral viewpoints and evolve a worldwide system of television and radio for information and education. We thus call for full international cooperation in culture, science, the arts, and technology *across ideological borders.* We must learn to live openly together or we shall perish together.

Humanity as a Whole

In closing: The world cannot wait for a reconciliation of competing political or economic systems to solve its problems. These are the times for men and women of good will to further the building of a peaceful and prosperous world. We urge that parochial loyalties and inflexible moral and religious ideologies be transcended. We urge recognition of the common humanity of all people. We further urge the use of reason and compassion to produce the kind of world we want—a world in which peace, prosperity, freedom, and happiness are widely shared. Let us not abandon that vision in despair or cowardice. We are responsible for what we are or will be. Let us work together for a humane world by means commensurate with humane ends. Destructive ideological differences among communism, capitalism, socialism, conservatism, liberalism, and radicalism should be overcome. Let us call for an end to terror and hatred. We will survive and prosper only in a world of shared humane values. We can initiate new directions for humankind; ancient rivalries can be superseded by broad-based cooperative efforts. The commitment to tolerance, understanding, and peaceful negotiation does not necessitate acquiescence to the status quo nor the damming up of dynamic and revolutionary forces. The true revolution is occurring and can continue in countless non-violent adjustments. But this entails the willingness to step forward onto new and expanding plateaus. At the present juncture of history, commitment to all humankind is the highest commitment of which we are capable; it transcends the narrow allegiances of church, state, party, class, or race in moving toward a wider vision of human potentiality. What more daring a goal for humankind than for each person to become, in ideal as well as practice, a citizen of a world community. It is a classical vision; we can now give it new vitality. Humanism thus interpreted is a moral force that has time on its side. We believe that humankind has the potential intelligence, good will, and cooperative skill to implement this commitment in the decades ahead.

We, the undersigned, while not necessarily endorsing every detail of the above, pledge our general support to *Humanist Manifesto II* for the future of humankind. These affirmations are not a final credo or dogma but an expression of a living and growing faith. We invite others in all lands to join us in further developing and working for these goals.

Lionel Abel, *Prof. of English, State Univ. of New York at Buffalo*
Khoren Arisian, *Board of Leaders, NY Soc. for Ethical Culture*
Isaac Asimov, *author*
George Axtelle, *Prof. Emeritus, Southern Illinois Univ.*
Archie J. Bahm, *Prof. of Philosophy Emeritus, Univ. of N.M.*
Paul H. Beattie, *Pres., Fellowship of Religious Humanists*
Keith Beggs, *Exec. Dir., American Humanist Association*
Malcolm Bissell, *Prof. Emeritus, Univ. of Southern California*
H. J. Blackham, *Chm., Social Morality Council, Great Britain*
Brand Blanshard, *Prof. Emeritus, Yale University*
Paul Blanshard, *author*
Joseph L. Blau, *Prof. of Religion, Columbia University*
Sir Hermann Bondi, *Prof. of Math., King's Coll., Univ. of London*
Howard Box, *Leader, Brooklyn Society for Ethical Culture*
Raymond B. Bragg, *Minister Emer., Unitarian Ch., Kansas City*
Theodore Brameld, *Visiting Prof., C.U.N.Y.*
Lester R. Brown, *Senior Fellow, Overseas Development Council*
Bette Chambers, *Pres., American Humanist Association*
John Ciardi, *poet*
Francis Crick, *M.D., Great Britain*
Arthur Danto, *Prof. of Philosophy, Columbia University*
Lucien de Coninck, *Prof., University of Gand, Belgium*
Miriam Allen deFord, *author*
Edd Doerr, *Americans United for Separation of Church and State*
Peter Draper, *M.D., Guy's Hospital Medical School, London*
Paul Edwards, *Prof. of Philosophy, Brooklyn College*
Albert Ellis, *Exec. Dir., Inst. Adv. Study Rational Psychotherapy*
Edward L. Ericson, *Board of Leaders, NY Soc. for Ethical Culture*
H. J. Eysenck, *Prof. of Psychology, Univ. of London*
Roy P. Fairfield, *Coordinator, Union Graduate School*
Herbert Feigl, *Prof. Emeritus, Univ. of Minnesota*

26

Additional Signers

Gina Allen, *author*

John C. Anderson, *Humanist Counselor*

Peter O. Anderson, *Assistant Professor, Ohio State University*

William F. Anderson, *Humanist Counselor*

John Anton, *Professor, Emory University*

Sir Alfred Ayer, *Professor, Oxford, Great Britain*

Celia Baker

Ernest Baker, *Associate Professor, University of the Pacific*

Marjorie S. Baker, *Ph.D., Pres., Humanist Community of San Francisco*

Henry S. Basayne, *Assoc. Exec. Off., Assn. for Humanistic Psych.*

Walter Behrendt, *Vice Pres., European Parliament, W. Germany*

Mildred H. Blum, *Secy., American Ethical Union*

W. Bonness, *Pres., Bund Freirelgioser Gemeinden, West Germany*

Robert O. Boothe, *Prof. Emer., Cal. Polytechnic*

Clement A. Bosch

Madeline L. Bosch

Bruni Boyd, *Vice Pres., American Ethical Union*

J. Lloyd Brereton, *ed.,* Humanist in Canada

Nancy Brewer, *Humanist Counselor*

D. Bronder, *Bund Freirelgioser Gemeinden, West Germany*

Charles Brownfield, *Asst. Prof., Queensborough Community College, CUNY*

Costantia Brownfield, *R.N.*

Margaret Brown, *Assoc. Prof., Oneonta State Univ. College*

Beulah L. Bullard, *Humanist Counselor*

Joseph Chuman, *Leader, Ethical Soc. of Essex Co.*

Gordon Clanton, *Asst. Prof., Trenton State College*

Daniel S. Collins, *Leader, Unitarian Fellowship of Jonesboro, Ark.*

Wm. Creque, *Pres., Fellowship of Humanity, Oakland, Ca.*

M. Benjamin Dell, *Dir., Amer. Humanist Assn.*

James Durant IV, *Prof., Polk Comm. College Winter Haven, Fla.*

Gerald A. Ehrenreich, *Assoc. Prof., Univ. of Kansas School of Medicine*

Marie Erdmann, *Teacher, Campbell Elementary School*

Robert L. Erdmann, *Ph.D., IBM*

Hans S. Falck, *Disting. Professor, Menninger Foundation*

James Farmer, *Director, Public Policy Training Institute*

Ed Farrar

Joe Felmet, *Humanist Counselor*

Thomas Ferrick, *Leader, Ethical Society of Boston*

Norman Fleishman, *Exec. Vice Pres., Planned Parenthood World Population, Los Angeles*

Joseph Fletcher, *Visiting Prof., Sch. of Medicine, Univ. of Virginia*

Douglas Frazier, *Leader, American Ethical Union*

Betty Friedan, *Founder, N.O.W.*

Harry M. Geduld, *Professor, Indiana University*

Roland Gibson, *President, Art Foundation of Potsdam, N.Y.*

Aron S. Gilmartin, *Minister, Mt. Diablo Unitarian Church, Walnut Creek, Ca.*

Annabelle Glasser, *Director, American Ethical Union*

Rebecca Goldblum, *Director, American Ethical Union*

Louis R. Gomberg, *Humanist Counselor*

Harold N. Gordon, *Vice President, American Ethical Union*

Sol Gordon, *Professor, Syracuse University*

Theresa Gould, *American Ethical Union*

Gregory O. Grant, *Captain, USAF*

Ronald Green, *Asst. Professor, New York University*

LeRue Grim, *Secretary, American Humanist Association*

S. Spencer Grin, *Publisher,* Saturday Review/World

Josephine R. Gurbarg, *Secy., Humanist Society of Greater Philadelphia*

Samuel J. Gurbarg

Lewis M. Gubrud, *Executive Director, Mediator Fellowship, Providence, R.I.*

Frank A. Hall, *Minister, Murray Univ. Church, Attleboro, Mass.*

Harold Hansen, *President, Space Coast Chapter, AHA*

Abul Hasanat, *Secretary, Bangladesh Humanist Society*

Ethelbert Haskins, *Director, American Humanist Association*

Lester H. Hayes, *Public Relations Director, American Income Life Insurance Company*

Donald E. Henshaw, *Humanist Counselor*

Alex Hershaft, *Principal Scientist, Booz Allen Applied Research*

Ronald E. Hestand, *author and columnist*

Irving Louis Horowitz, *editor,* Society

Warren S. Hoskins, *Humanist Counselor*

Mark W. Huber, *Director, American Ethical Union*

Harold J. Hutchison, *Humanist Counselor*

Sir Julian Huxley, *former head, UNESCO, Great Britain*
Arthur M. Jackson, *Exec. Dir., Humanist Community of San Jose;
Treasurer, American Humanist Association*
Linda R. Jackson, *Director, American Humanist Association*
Steven Jacobs, *former President, American Ethical Union*
Thomas B. Johnson, Jr., *consulting psychologist*
Robert Edward Jones, *Exec. Dir., Joint Washington Office for
Social Concern*
Marion Kahn, *Pres., Humanist Society of Metropolitan New York*
Alec E. Kelley, *Professor, University of Arizona*
Marvin Kohl, *Professor, SUNY at Fredonia*
Frederick C. Kramer, *Humanist Counselor*
Eugene Kreves, *Minister, DuPage Unit. Church, Naperville, Ill.*
Pierre Lamarque, *France*
Helen B. Lamb, *economist*
Jerome D. Lang, *Pres., Humanist Assoc. of Greater Miami, Fla.*
Harvey Lebrun, *Chairman, Chapter Assembly, AHA*
Helen Leibson, *President, Philadelphia Ethical Society*
John F. MacEnulty, Jr., *Pres., Humanist Soc. of Jacksonville, Fla.*
James T. McCollum, *Humanist Counselor*
Vashti McCollum, *former President of AHA*
Russell L. McKnight, *Pres., Humanist Association of Los Angeles*
Ludlow P. Mahan, Jr., *Pres., Humanist Chapter of Rhode Island*
Andrew Malleson, *M.D., psychiatrist*
Clem Martin, *M.D.*
James R. Martin, *Humanist Counselor*
Stanley E. Mayabb, *Co-Fndr.: Humanist Group of Vacaville and
Men's Colony, San Luis Obispo*
Zhores Medvedev, *scientist, U.S.S.R.*
Abelardo Mena, *M.D., senior psychiatrist, V. A. Hospital,
Miami, Fla.*
Jacques Monod, *Institut Pasteur, France*
Herbert J. Muller, *Professor, University of Indiana*
Robert J. Myler, *Title Officer, Title Insurance & Trust Company*
Gunnar Myrdal, *Professor, University of Stockholm, Sweden*
H. Kyle Nagel, *Minister, Unit. Univ. Church of Kinston, N.C.*
Dorothy N. Naiman, *Professor Emerita, Lehman College, CUNY*
Muriel Neufeld, *Executive Committee, American Ethical Union*
Walter B. Neumann, *Treasurer, American Ethical Union*
G. D. Parikh, *Indian Radical Humanist Association, India*

Eleanor Wright Pelrine, *author, Canada*
Bernard Porter, *President, Toronto Humanist Association*
William Earl Proctor, Jr., *President, Philadelphia area, AHA*
Gonzalo Quiogue, *Vice Pres., Humanist Assn. of the Philippines*
James A. Rafferty, *Lecturer, USIU School of Human Behavior*
Anthony F. Rand, *President, Humanist Society of Greater Detroit*
A. Philip Randolph, *President, A. Philip Randolph Institute*
Ruth Dickinson Reams, *President, Humanist Association
National Capital Area*
Jean-Francois Revel, *journalist, France*
Bernard L. Riback, *Humanist Counselor*
B. T. Rocca, Sr., *President, United Secularists of America*
M. L. Rosenthal, *Professor, New York University*
Jack C. Rubenstein, *Executive Committee, AEU*
Joseph R. Sanders, *Professor, University of West Florida*
William Schulz, *Ph.D. cand., Meadville/
Lombard, Univ. of Chicago*
Walter G. Schwartz, *Dir., Humanist Comm. of
San Francisco*
John W. Sears, *clinical psychologist*
Naomi Shaw, *Pres., National Women's Conference, AEU*
R. L. Shuford, III, *Instructor, Charlotte Country
Day School*
Sidney Siller, *Chm, Comm. for Fair Divorce and Alimony Laws*
Joell Silverman, *Chm., Religious Education Committee, AEU*
Warren A. Smith, *Pres., Variety Sound Corp.*
A. Solomon, *coordinator, Indian Secular Society*
Robert Sone
Robert M. Stein, *Co-Chairman, Public Affairs Committee, AEU*
Stuart Stein, *Director, American Ethical Union*
Arnold E. Sylvester
Emerson Symonds, *Director, Sensory Awareness Center*
Carolyn Symonds, *marriage counselor*
Ward Tabler, *Visiting Professor, Starr King School*
Barbara M. Tabler
V. M. Tarkunde, *Pres., All Indian Radical Humanist Assn., India*
Erwin Theobold, *Instructor, Pasadena City College*
Ernest N. Ukpaby, *Dean, University of Nigeria*
Renate Vambery, *Ethical Soc. of St. Louis, President, AHA
St. Louis Chapter*
Nick D. Vasileff, *St. Louis Ethical Society*

Robert J. Wellman, *Humanist Chaplain, C. W. Post Center, Long Island University*
May H. Weis, *UN Representative for IHEU*
Paul D. Weston, *Leader, Ethical Culture Society of Bergen County*
Georgia H. Wilson, *retired, Political Sc. Dept., Brooklyn College*
H. Van Rensselaer Wilson, *Prof., Emer., Brooklyn College*
James E. Woodrow, *Exec. Dir., Asgard Enterprises, Inc.*

Note: If you would like to sign Humanist Manifesto II, please send your name and address to:

The Humanist *Magazine*
923 Kensington Ave.
Buffalo, New York 14215